Jumping The Rope

Move Yourself and Manifest Your Success

Bernadette Henry

The Writers Game

Jumping The Rope

Move Yourself and Manifest Your Success

Bernadette Henry

The Writers Game

"*The moment you begin to prioritize yourself, your dreams and the vision that you were put onto this earth to accomplish, is the same moment you realize your true power.*"

- Bernadette Henry

Disclaimer

This book is for educational purposes only. The views expressed are those of the author alone. The reader is responsible for his or her own actions. Adherence to all applicable laws and regulations, including international, federal, state and local governing professional licensing, business practices, advertising and all other aspects of doing business in The United States, Canada or any other jurisdiction is the sole responsibility of the purchaser or reader. Neither the author nor the publisher assumes any responsibility or liability whatsoever on the behalf of the purchasers or reader of these materials.

JUMPING THE ROPE

The Writers Game

8936 Northpointe Executive Park Drive, Ste 260,

Huntersville, NC 28078

info@thewritersgame.com

www.thewritersgame.com

ISBN: 979-8-9875189-2-2

eBook ISBN: 979-8-9875189-3-9

Printed in The United States of America

Contents

To the woman that stopped believing in a better landing, this book is dedicated to remind you that what you've experienced is everything you need to empower the power inside of you. Continue to push, continue to fight and continue to JUMP the rope.

To all that inspired, coached, challenged and empowered me in any way, I thank you for your tireless service, time and blessing. Without you, I wouldn't have the opportunity to empower others.

JUMPING THE ROPE

"Jump rope isn't about jumping, it's about finding the right rhythm and being free. I guess life is a lot like jump rope; we must stop thinking and find our rhythm too." - Bernadette Henry

What could only take a few seconds of time and action, most people spend their whole lives waiting inactively on the right moment to take their first jump. See the jumping I want you to envision at this moment has nothing to do with proper form, genetics, or even the right timing like we may visualize in various sporting events or fitness exercises. The jumping I am describing is much different and takes only one characteristic that is much more powerful than any of the other abilities mentioned above, yet the biggest difference is it is universal in nature and every single person on earth has it right now.

You know what that is, the characteristic of courage. It may take genetics and athletic ability to slam dunk a basketball, a bit of skill to properly dive into a pool from a higher altitude, and much preparation to jump out of a plane but all it takes is courage when you are wanting to take your first real jump into the abyss of achievement, the pool of purpose, and reach the mountaintop of manifestation.

Why does it take us our whole lives to stand up for the beliefs and values that we have, finally begin pursuing the career that we want, or begin operating in the gifts that we've been born with? The answers I have frequently heard is that it is not the right timing, I don't have the support, or my favorite one yet, I need more money before I start. In this book, JUMP, Move Yourself and Manifest Your Success, I am going to show you that what you have been telling yourself all of this time are not reasons, they are serving as barriers that are blocking the success, joy, and peace that you desperately deserve and have been patiently waiting for.

Whether you are the mother that has given up dreams of becoming a surgeon because you have redirected your focus to raise your children, it is time for you to JUMP.

Whether you are the college graduate that went the corporate America route rather than finalizing your invention that you worked on all through college to appease your parents, it is time for you to JUMP.

Whether you are that seasoned entrepreneur or successful business owner that wants something different but doesn't know what different looks like because your identity is wrapped up in your bottom line, it is time for you to JUMP.

Whether you are that young man that is in love with your partner, but fears getting married too early, it is time for you to JUMP.

The world believes that jumping takes hand eye coordination, strength, stamina, and all of these abilities that take time to learn, but the jumping I am describing to you throughout this book takes courage and for you to stand up for your success, plant your feet in your purpose, and not allow any storm to move you away from the mission that you were put onto this world to accomplish. The same courage it took you to pick up this book and begin reading, is the same level of courage it will take for you to pick back up your dream that has collected dust for so long and begin working on it and walking towards it.

Journey of The Underdog Making Progress

Everyone loves watching a good underdog story, but no one likes to be the underdog, face downtrodden circumstances, and remain committed to rising against impossible odds. The term " J.U.M.P. " is characterized through this book as the journey of the underdog making progress. Through this book, it's the goal to commit to improvement without letting the idea of perfection diminish the value that you have inside of you. You've already taken a significant step in deciding to take action and read this book, and through the rest of the book, I hope that we answer the question, "what is the next step I need to take?" Whether you have been the underdog in the past or are currently in a season where you realize that you have been overlooked or cast out, I hope that through the pages of this book, I assist you with the steps necessary to make to be confident, comfortable and courageous before you JUMP.

Your First Step Begins Here:

It said that a journey of a thousand miles, starts with taking your first step. If you were to think of your dream being that thousand mile journey, right now I want you to write down what would be the first step you need to take so that every day is an intentional leap towards the legacy that you want to leave once you are no longer able to step forward.

My First Step Is:

_____

_____

_____

They say the hardest part of any transformation is just taking the first step, but I challenge this theory. It is easy starting the idea, getting into the relationship, or even writing down the business plan. The real challenges come for me throughout my journey as well as so many others is when the initial plan doesn't work, the relationship begins to experience difficulty, or the idea doesn't seem to be as "innovative" as you once thought it would be. The real courage comes not only in taking the first step, but being committed to knowing once the step does not go as planned, having the character to commit to the best next step to follow.

Throughout the pages inside this book, you will soon learn that I was just like you in so many ways; operating in fear which was ultimately leading to my mission not being able to operate in my life. I was scared of becoming the woman I am today and the woman I am destined to be, because at first I did not know who that person was. I was so connected to who the world believed I deserved to be, that I never took the time thinking, visualizing and learning what I believed God wanted from me, what I envisioned for my life, and who I wanted to become. In the chapters of this book, you will continue to answer the question, "who I am next, what do I do now" so that you can have a full understanding and realize that who you want to become in the next season, takes action in this current moment.

Who Am I Next:

Answer the question on who do you want to become in this next season or chapter of your life. Visualize that person and who you want to become.

_____

_____

_____

What Do I Do Now:

Answer what is the first step that needs to take place in order to become that person. The quicker that you embody the characteristics, the quicker you'll inherit the rewards.

_____

_____

_____

Imagine if you committed to this process on a daily, weekly or consistent basis of reflection and internal course correction; who do you believe you'd be able to become? What do you believe you'd be able to accomplish? The challenge that I have faced and so many of us are currently experiencing as we are reading this book is that we continue to move forward and not take the intentional time assessing our circumstance, actions and choices while shaming ourselves for not being exactly where we envision. We must commit to meeting every punch that is thrown, not with more grit, but more grace allowing us to feel the blow's impact, while being prepared to ready the counter every time.

When life throws you a blow, counter it with grace every time and you will make it through the rest of the match, I guarantee it.

This next season will be your best season and it is time for you to receive everything you deserve. You deserve to experience and feel love, joy and a deeper peace consistently. You deserve to receive praise for your accomplishments and innovations. You deserve to be free of debt, financial obligation and be secure and able to make lifestyle decisions that don't stress you out. You deserve to feel free in your life, household and in your decisions that you feel are right. All it takes is jumping with courage, staying consistent and committed to your process, course correcting through your journey and countering each blow with grace.

It took me almost forty years to produce what you will read inside these 200 pages and I am thankful for your support, commitment, but most of all, you jumping.

I look forward to your transformation, I hope you are ready to JUMP, MOVE, and MANIFEST YOUR SUCCESS.

Know More to Jump The Rope

JUMPING takes only one characteristic, and that is COURAGE.

What is Your First Step NOW that can help you become who you want to be NEXT? Taking small short steps will help you on this journey of a thousand miles.

Reflection through your process allows you to course correct your plane's route consistently. Check your actions and habits consistently so you know when to alter anything in our life.

Counter every blow that you may take with grace, every time.

Feelings, Reflections and Actions

Use the pages below to write your feelings or reflections from the chapter or take this time to write out your action plan to begin YOUR BECOMING JOURNEY.

_____

_____

_____

_____

_____

_____

_____

_____

_____

_____

_____

_____

_____

_____

_____

_____

_____

_____

_____

_____

_____

_____

_____

_____

_____

_____

_____

_____

_____

_____

_____

_____

_____

BERNADETTE HENRY

Chapter 1

FORGIVING WHAT YOU CAN'T FORGET

"To forgive is to set a prisoner free and discover that the prisoner was you all along." - Lewis B. Smedes

I heard a quote once that said, "When the storm comes we can either go around it or go through it, but we best not wait until the storm comes to our door because it is then too late to take action." Taking intentional action to navigate the high tides that storms bring is a skill and there is an art to being fully prepared for these instances in our lives. Whether you have perceived certain situations in your life as a storm or need a bit of help identifying what maybe these instances are, it is important to understand everybody is going to experience different levels of storms on their journey towards purpose.

Whether that storm is a loss of a loved one, a trauma that causes you to take a break or time to make a course correction, or whether it is burnout or depression, there are so many different categories of storms that you either have or will experience, so being aware of what these look like, what you need, and how you can respond are essential to bringing not only yourself but your ship and crew to shore safely.

I loved this quote when I first heard it and I still love it now because it encompasses so much within one sentence, and that is whatever you do during these times, to take action and not remain stagnant waiting for anything to come to you. I've heard and witnessed so many friends, colleagues, peers and even people that I admire communicate their desires, but when you ask them what they are doing to work on it, there isn't any intention behind the words and a course of action that will allow them to reach that place. Denzel Washington quotes, "Dreams without goals are simply ideas that amass to nothing if not acted on." The same is true with anything you are communicating and without intentional action and commitment it's simply words and sounds that will not lead to any feeling of success.

Similar to most quotes they are providing amazing wisdom in the moment and theories that we can recite with no real blueprint on the best course of implementation that will aid us in proceeding forward and getting one step closer to the light at the end of the tunnel.

In this chapter, we want you prepared to navigate your sail through the various storms that will come during your journey on the ocean of creating better opportunities in your life. You will be prepared to navigate both high and low tides and make it to the shores of success and feel proud that you not only made it through each storm, but you were more prepared and equipped to navigate any storm that may come in the future.

Questions that I frequently hear that you may be asking or have asked yourself in the past are:

How do I identify the storm?

How do I prepare for the storm prior to it coming?

How do I go through the storm or around the storm and come out stronger?

What happens if the storm just ends up at my door, how do I best respond?

All of these questions can be answered if we examine three major components such as the ability to read your compass, your ship's condition, and your ship's crew members.

Ability to Read Your Compass

If you were dropped off in a forest 10 miles from your home with nothing but a compass, do you believe you'd be able to effectively find your way home? Most of us would humbly and honestly not be able to make it home safely and it would take a rescue party and a miracle to be able to bring us back home. This is the same in life as well, because sometimes we can't remember why we ended up where we are, but I believe our internal compass, is the discernment, gut feeling and little voice inside that is continuing to speak to us but our ability to read and listen to this compass, will determine our success or failure in making it to our destination while we are sailing.

During the toughest storms, the first thing that often cuts out is the power and without power we can't have the privilege of all the technological advances that may be giving us certain advantages. Your ability to read a compass and have full clarity on where you are going, what you want, and how you can still follow your north star is absolutely critical to you being able to lead your ship, its people and yourself towards the shoreline of success.

The Ship's Condition

It doesn't matter how good a crew or ship's captain may be, if the ship is in terrible condition it will not be able to withstand the storms that will come through this journey. It doesn't matter how amazing your idea, how great your innovation, how successful your business, if you are not taking care of your health, your mind, your relationships, and your ship will not make it to the shore. Ships don't sink because of the water around them, they sink because of the water that stays inside them, and we have to assess the holes or repairs that need to be made to the ship prior to taking the ship to sea.

We will talk throughout this whole book about "jumping" and the courage that it takes to take action, but before you are able to jump, I want you to check in on your ships condition and ask yourself if you are physically, mentally, emotionally, spiritually and even financially ready and have the capacity to jump during this time.

I'd rather you risk a little bit of time and prepare your ship for travel, rather than risk your life and the lives of others going to sea with a broken down ship that should have never been in the ocean. What are things that you have been putting off that will cause your ship to sink once it is taken out to shore?

Ship's Crew Members

A restaurant is only as good as its chefs, an airline is only as good as its pilots and your journey will be only as good as your crew members that you take to sea with you. As much as I would love to say that this journey is one that you can take alone and it will only take you and you only, I would be lying to you because that is where most people make the mistake. The journey of a thousand miles may start with your ideas and your steps, but will eventually need someone else's affirmation, push, and expertise to help you push through the finish line. In this section it isn't about telling you about who these people would need to be in your life, but I will help by posing this question.

When you think about the person you are working to become, who does that person need and who is absolutely essential to that person in order for them to feel joyful, peaceful, and prepared?

Write down 3-5 people below:

_____

_____

_____

Congratulations, you just built your crew list for your first destination and journey. This is either going to do two things, excite you because you are one step closer to going to the sea and taking on that storm head on, or frustrate you, because you recognize that the current relationships that you have may not be the best choices for the destination ahead. Remember what we said in the previous chapter, for every blow that comes up, counter it with grace every time. If the relationships don't align, that is okay, but it is not okay to have the wrong people on the right path because you are not going to end up in the right destination at the end. I've battled with this where I've recognized that certain relationships, friendships, and even loved ones were not best fit for where I was going, until I remembered that every jump starts with courage not only to take the action, but to commit to the process that follows.

Once we've done an assessment on our ship's condition, our ability to follow a compass and brought on our new crew members, it is time for us to take sail. Before you sail, I don't want you to look back, I don't want you pushing your sails down for the wind to catch it and realize you have anchors that are still keeping you connected to the dock. After you decide, it is time to release the fear, judgment, and shame that you feel from leaving anyone behind and trust that little inner voice inside directing you forward.

In every transition that I experienced, I also experienced a easy path back to comfortability, back to circumstance and back to the person that I was walking away from inviting me back to the playground to play, the bar to drink or to the bedroom to commit to activities that once were acceptable to ultimately look back and recognize they weren't allowing me to progress forward. One thing that I've learned through this sailing journey is that there are some storms that you can not avoid and even if you have prepared your environment there are still some storms that come, that drench you and force you to start over. My storm came before I realized it was a storm and years ago, a series of events plagued my emotions, threatened my integrity and stole my innocence before I was even of age to have the courage to speak up and speak out on the events that for most women we don't recover from.

Trauma in my opinion is anything that happens to you that is uncomfortable and shakes your emotions, threatens your perspective and puts you in a position of vulnerability before you are equipped with the tools to navigate the events and instances that lead up to it. Whether being embarrassed in public, to being sexually assaulted, to being potentially bullied at school, we can not minimize people's responses to trauma, and we must normalize how we begin to identify triggers that can help us put defense mechanisms in place that will help for us not to repeat them.

What has worked for generations before you today, may not work for you in the events that you experience, so following the method below will help you navigate through tragedy and have techniques to heal forward properly. It is true and scientifically proven that trauma is passed down from generation directly or indirectly. What may have been normal in your household, you may grow to learn that is unacceptable as an adult as you cultivate new formed opinions, beliefs and values. Before we can successfully and effectively incorporate others into our lives, it is important for us to learn the patterns, triggers, and root causes of certain feelings that we are experiencing so we can reshape the environment before we react to the event. This consistently takes a commitment to reflection, understanding and being willing to learn and grow through your process. Follow the three steps listed below to help you recreate your environments in a way that empower you and not anchor you to what you are trying to walk away from.

Your Trauma is Not Your Fault

All of us reading this book have probably some time in our life have heard the phrase, "get over it," "you'll be fine," or my favorite, "life happens." As much as I want to challenge all three of these phrases and tell you to immediately remove them from your vocabulary, I'd be remiss if I wasn't honest in saying that I've even been unaware of the damaging effects when I've used them myself.

It is true that life does happen and eventually through time, you will be able to get over the circumstance and be back operationally, but that doesn't mean that you have successfully gotten through what you experienced or healed appropriately in a way that will allow you to experience the feelings that you deserve.

Just because you put a bandaid over a wound and keep stopping the blood temporarily doesn't;'t mean you have healed the underlying infection that may be arising. The same happens in life when we experience hurtful situations that cut into our emotions and feelings deep and even though we've been conditioned to use bandaids, a hint of alcohol and Neosporin, it doesn't mean that it is the best solution to heal what has been damaged. The first step when you experience these moments, is to not blame yourself and as we mentioned in the previous chapters use grace as your counterpunch before and know immediately that you've been equip with the compass, the crew and you already are aware of your ships condition to know that you have everything you need to prevail.

Accept what has occurred as part of your journey as you are sailing and recognize that some storms may last for hours, days and even weeks, but no storm will persist forever. Your feelings matter and they may last for an extended period of time, but do trust that what you feel during that moment of discomfort is what is developing that stamina, strength and muscle memory that is equipping and empowering the expert captain that you are as you are navigating the high tides. Once you've accepted your experience and met tragedy at the gate, I want you to write down three to five affirmations that you will commit to communicating daily that will be a part of your daily routine.

What are three to five affirmations if life knocked you in the mouth that you would need to hear daily to help you keep going?

Write 3-5 Affirmations Below:

_____

_____

_____

Meet instances with an affirmation and trust yourself and the little voice inside that will serve as your compass through your journey. You are equipped with the stamina, strength and smarts to be able to navigate this storm and get your ship to shore safely. Remember that some storms may have an extended stay, but they don't ever stay forever.

Acknowledge and Take Time To You

Despite what anyone says, thinks or feels, your feelings, emotions and how you respond to any circumstance in your life matter and deserve the space, time and environment to be navigated appropriately. What this looks like with different people, depending on different circumstances is different for everyone that may be reading so I want to have you try something that may help you understand what to do when you are in one of these anchoring moments. A trick that I commit to each time I feel myself falling off my rocker is asking myself five questions:

1. What do I feel right now and what does this feeling mean?

2. Why does this feeling feel like this and what is the root of my feelings?

3. What feeling do I want to feel that will help me become the best version of myself for tomorrow?

4. What can I do to love, empower, and support myself today that will bring me joy, peace and happiness?

5. How much time do I need and what will I do in this time to keep me moving forward?

Acknowledging and assessing the experience and feeling will allow you to best pathway forward towards experiencing what you desire. Take as much time as you need and do not go through this alone. Whether you consult with a friend that is a part of your crew team or connect with a professional, don't ever think that you have to go through this alone.

The Journey of Healing

Like any journey or adventure, this journey of healing is just that, a journey and there is no race to the finish line because there isn't a finish line. Life doesn't get easier, you just get stronger and you learn how to navigate the high tides more appropriately in ways that support and empower you best.

My friend, I want you to not try to avoid feeling what you are feeling and don't try to numb the pain at all, the feeling of loss, disappointment, and heartbreak make the feeling of excitement, peace and joy so much more amazing when you don't numb the pain and sit in the feeling for a while. There is no quick fix, deadline, or expiration on your emotions, so we have to get out of the habit of rushing the process and allow your internal flower to bloom naturally. With any growth, it takes nourishment and nurturing, and it is the same with the growth process that you will be required to commit to through the process of being in a state of pain.

Follow these few questions below to begin mapping out what your journey of healing will look for you.

Finding Your Nourishment and Identifying What to Nurture

- Environment: What environments do I need to begin involving myself in order to be in a space of support, love, and empowerment?

- Sunlight: What activities can I do that light me up and bring me joy?

- Fertilizer: What are some relationships I need to cultivate that can assist me in moving forward towards my purpose?

- Soil: What are some values and boundaries I need to plant inside my heart so I can not repeat the same cycle?

- Water: What are certain things that I am consuming that need to be washed away?

- Time: What are self care activities I can commit to on a daily, weekly or monthly basis that can become a part of my regular routine?

Redesign Your Environment

The best way to heal is by surrounding yourself with people who love, nurture you, and support you even by way of challenging you. Cultivating relationships that feed your spirit, nurture your soul, and please your heart are hard to come by but when you find that tribe, do as much as you can to nurture those relationships. Your tribe is going to be the armor you need in order to help you progress past the pain and instead of taking those small steps on this road of a thousand miles, they will provide you the jolt of energy and power you need to begin taking larger leaps. As a part of redesigning your environment, it's not just about people, it's also about redesigning the places, perspectives and some habits that you may be used to.

Answer these questions below to help you navigate the need to redesign your environment:

1. Where do I need to stop going because it reminds me of the place that I am trying to get away from?

2. What are certain routines or habits that I have that don't promote growth and development?

3. What are thoughts I have about myself that don't promote love, joy and bring me peace?

4. Who are some people that remind me of who I used to be and it is time to begin moving away from those relationships?

Remember this, in every transition and transformation something will have to be sacrificed. You have to make the choice which sacrifices are more important; the dream that you have or the things that you cling to that keep you away from accomplishing the dream. I look forward to seeing you in the next chapter.

Know More to Jump The Rope

Give Yourself Permission to Let Go

- Create a positive mantra to counter any painful thoughts you may feel

- Allow the negative emotions to flow like a river but not sit like a lake

- Be gentle with yourself and give yourself grace ALWAYS

Take Time to Reflect on Which Past Experiences and Beliefs Are Affecting You Today

- If you feel it, write it down and reflect on what it represents now and what it represented then

- **Ask yourself:** "What is this feeling telling me about where I am and where I am going?"

Sit and Write Your Vision Map and Your Vision Blockers

- **Ask yourself:** "What do I deeply desire most in life right now and in the next 6-12 months?"

- **Ask yourself:** "What are the blockers in front of why I don't have that?"

Take Intentional and Consistent Actions On Changing Your Circumstance

- Your actions will determine WHO you will become and WHERE you will end up. Once you write the action, commit to the activity daily.

Feelings, Reflections and Actions

Use the pages below to write your feelings or reflections from the chapter or take this time to write out your action plan to begin YOUR BECOMING JOURNEY.

_____

_____

_____

_____

_____

_____

_____

_____

_____

_____

_____

_____

_____

_____

_____

Chapter 2

STOP TRIPPING OVER THE ROPE

"In the process of letting go you will lose many things from the past, but you will find yourself." - Deepak Chopra

The late Lewis B Smedes quotes, "to forgive is to set a prisoner free and discover that the prisoner was you all along." Have you ever felt like a prisoner in your own emotions, relationships or even in your own mind? Have you ever felt like every time you were trying to make that big leap it seemed like you kept tripping over the rope. In my experience over the years I have been a jump rope enthusiast, I realized that it may be one of three reasons that you may be tripping over the rope.

Maybe it's the length of the rope, height you're trying to jump or maybe the technique in which you are moving your arms. Either way, I understand the frustration that persists every time you feel you have to start over after trying to find your rhythm. Let's explore these three reasons a bit deeper below.

Length of The Rope

Whether your rope is too long or too short, having control of the length is necessary to making the jumps work in flow. In life everything has a length and expiration date. What worked for us in one season, may no longer serve us in the next chapter. One thing I want you to consider as you are reading through this chapter are things that helped you become successful in the past, but may not be effective as you enter new levels. When you begin to notice certain decisions, actions or habits as inactive, it's up to you to shorten the rope and take control of the next actions and choices in your life.

Height You Are Jumping

When I first started jumping rope, I used to jump so high in the air trying to tuck my knees to my chest. This is how a lot of us go into new opportunities and spaces within our lives. We are trying to jump high, take major leaps, and take big steps, much too early, not realizing that we just need to take steps high enough for the rope to pass underneath our feet. As you are reading through this chapter, continue to recognize that it is the smallest changes that set you up for the biggest transformations. What are some small habits that you're preparing to commit to in order to create massive change in your life?

Arm Technique

Remember that activity doesn't equal achievement in any area of your life. Just as excessive arm movement can lead to tripping of the rope in jump roping, action without any intention in life can lead to missed opportunities and disappointment. It is not about moving quickly, it's about being concise and correct in your decision making process. Be willing to commit to the process of learning, growing and empowering those around you. What are intentional activities that you can commit to on a daily basis that will always push the needle forward? Whether you are reading 5 pages of a book, working out for 30 minutes or finding time to meditate or pray, commit to a set of activities every day so that even if your day seems a bit unproductive, that deep down you know you were able to progress forward.

I have, like many of us, feared our physical freedoms being taken to us, but aren't intentionally setting boundaries that will create opportunities for our emotional and mental feelings to be stripped as well.

It's always been a fear of mine to make a choice that resulted in me being incarcerated because I have heard stories of the horrors that persist behind the bars as well as understand the consequences once someone leaves and how hard it is to transition back into society. We work so hard to follow laws, rules and become law abiding citizens in order to never put us in a position to be locked away and our freedoms snatched from us.

Once I realized I worked hard to not allow my physical bodies to be locked away, but I was a bit careless regarding my emotions and feelings, I knew it was time to make a massive shift and alter the activity that surrounded my life immediately.

In our previous chapter we explored the journey that one must take when they are dealt the blow. We created a progressive approach in order for you to acknowledge your feelings, accept the instance and events, all while activating the power within you in order to move through the circumstance and recognize that it is not stronger than the calling that's been placed on your life.

As I was writing the first draft of this book, I initially left out this chapter because I didn't believe it was going to be significant towards the overall message of moving forward as you are manifesting your success, until I realized one thing.

Feelings such as anger, frustration, heartbreak, aggravation, doubt and any feeling that we deem as negative are far from negative, they are all necessary to strengthen the emotional foundation and work to become more emotionally intelligent and proactive. Emotional intelligence isn't just a buzzword, it's an intention that we must set within our lives whether we are entering or exiting any relationship. Having a better understanding of ourselves will ultimately allow us to experience better relationships both personally and professionally within our lives. According to Daniel Goleman, an American psychologist who helped to popularize emotional intelligence, he described there are give key elements to emotional intelligence:

- Self Regulation

- Self Awareness

- Motivation

- Empathy

- Social Skills

Self Regulation

Verbally attacking, making rash or rushed emotional decisions, judging people or continuing to compromise on your values are all signs that there may need to be some work in the area of self regulation. In instances where you have allowed your emotions to get the best of you, know it happens and it is okay, but not repeating the cycle and implementing a few different tricks may help you better maintain relationships, manage your emotions, and have a much better outcome during certain situations moving forward. Do you have a clear understanding of what you believe and value in life? Whether it is honesty, accountability, or loyalty, do you have a set of values that you will not compromise on no matter the circumstance. I challenge you to begin with your values and in situations, before you respond, take a deep breath and ask yourself does this promote my values or move me away from what I value. Once we understand our values and what is most important to us, it allows us to hold ourselves account-able and be proactive rather than reactive in our responses.

Self Awareness

Knowing what is happening and how to respond is one thing, but knowing how it is making you feel and being aware enough to identify triggers, slow down to make decisions, and having the strength to make sound choices is a level of awareness that will help you progress forward in all areas of your life. Over the years, journaling my thoughts, experiences, wants, challenges and deepest fears has allowed me to see on paper where I currently exist in the world and allows me to know the gap between where I currently am and where I desire to be. Throughout this book we've provided pages for you to follow along with the text as well as use this time during your reading to write and reflect on your own experiences. Every day towards the end of your day, I recommend taking 10-15 minutes to journal how you are feeling, what made you happy, what created more tense feelings, what is it that you want and do not want. Get in the habit of taking control of your life by first slowing down your life and examining what is actually going on.

Motivation

The truth about motivation is that you will not always feel inspired, motivated or lead to consistently work towards your goal, so it is important when motivation begins to dwindle down you remain disciplined and committed to your activity. It is said that as you grow, distractions are disguised in new opportunities so be wary of agreeing to opportunities that sound great in the moment, that will distract you from focusing on your mission at hand. Consistently ask yourself, "why," you're doing this and challenge yourself to remain on a path that only promotes where you are going and not allowing you to be "stagnate" in perceived success without progressing towards your purpose. Every time you may encounter a challenge, find the lesson in every situation and add it to your wisdom notebook as you are continuing to take steps forward. Through pain, inconvenience and discomfort, perspective and power is born.

Empathy

Showing empathy and having compassion is one of the hardest characteristics to develop, because it takes humility, patience and a commitment to understanding the point of view of someone else rather than your own. When you begin to look at situations from other people's perspectives, begin paying attention to social cues and body language and understand how to respond and engage differently based upon you empathizing with people, it allows you to create much better situations, responses and environments with the people in your life. So often, we have a "me, me, me," approach, but when engaging with other people I challenge you to put you to the side for a moment to learn more about how the other person feels, what the other person perceives and how the other person is affected, before finding the best course of action during the situation. When in doubt, ask better questions and remove the assumption and judgment.

Social Skills

From a scale 1-10, 1 being not very good to, to 10, absolutely amazing; how well do you manage the relationships in your life? Have you set clear boundaries and are you able to be free, honest and fluid in interactions or are there deep feelings of discomfort, lack of trust and a wall up because you don't feel comfortable expressing your needs, wants, desires and expectations for that relationship? Managing relationships where both parties feel loved, supported and cared for is challenging if honesty and clear communication isn't at the foundation of the relationship. Be willing to communicate what you desire, what can not work for you as well as what you need from that relationship and be willing to listen to what they also need from you. Schedule in temperature checks to make sure that different things haven't changed in the relationship and as each of you grow, that the relationship continues to grow as well.

The feeling of devastation, disappointment and anger that we were discussing earlier are normal and I hope you remain connected with the techniques that are shared throughout the remainder of the chapter. These feelings are real and happen, but as you become aware of your triggers and what is causing them, you are able to approach situations differently with intelligence and preparation rather than emotional reactions.

Until I recognized and came to terms that the anger that I felt towards my own family and church family for telling me to "get over," the tragedy of being molested as an adolescent continuously and not being taken serious, haunted me for years serving as the cloud that stayed on top of my head even on the most shiny summer days.

Even on days when I wanted to be happy, there were so many parts of me that I couldn't smile or even when I smiled it wasn't a feeling of joy it served as a shield so that people wouldn't see my open scars. I had so many people around me in my presence, but I felt alone emotionally and that I didn't have anywhere that I could go that was safe, secure where I was seen.

It was a cloud that lasted for too long and in this cloud it was filled with anger towards people for minimizing my trauma, shame towards myself for disappointing decisions, and disappointment for not meeting or exceeding the expectations that I knew I had the right to achieve.

The longer that I held onto all of those feelings, it continued to prolonged all of the feelings of love, peace, joy and happiness that I knew I deserved, but because I was holding onto the pain instead of meeting it and countering it with grace, I wasn't able to move forward and I was locked up in a prison to find out years later that I had the key in my hand the whole time. Stop allowing temporary situations to result in a life sentence.

Ask yourself these three questions to reflect where you are right now:

1. What was the crime (event) that has put you into prison?

2. What could both parties have done differently or better to avoid the infraction?

3. What damages were caused during the crime (event) that need time to heal or be repaired?

4. What is the best repair plan in order to get you back on the road as quickly as possible?

Not dealing with a painful plague of shame, grief and anger doesn't just affect you, it will soon lead to infecting the people closest to you and ultimately it finds itself being the cause for us not believing in ourselves, being able to trust people as well as being open to experiencing love again. Throughout this chapter you'll learn a few different methods. I've both learned and applied in my life when the anger and feelings begin to creep in that I don't want to consume the potential of reaching the calling we are on the journey working to obtain.

As we referenced towards the end of our last chapter, asking yourself the question of "What perspectives and feelings that you need to wash away in order for you to experience what's necessary to push you into the next season," will allow you to reflect on what is in the way of where you are destined to end up.

Untangling The Connection

It is important throughout this journey of transformation and transition that we be comfortable with disconnecting with the world's standard and reconnecting with ourselves in solitude. In order for us to jump naturally, we can't have the rope tangled because it will continue to interfere with the flow and rhythm of every single jump that follows after. Untangle, unwind and let go of all the people, beliefs, and areas in your life that you are connected to that interfere with who you are trying to become. Through this chapter we have discussed what emotional intelligence is and how we can implement it in our lives. With becoming more intelligent and intuitive, it's not only about identifying the positive desires, it is all about being mindful of the challenges and negative characteristics that we have that potentially lead to detrimental cycles and unhealthy behaviors and relationships. It's just as important to hold yourself accountable as much as you want to hold the people accountable in your life, and we do this by first reflecting on what is currently tangled in our rope.

List 3-5 Perspectives, Beliefs, People, Environments That You Believe Are Consistently Tangling Your Rope:

_____

_____

_____

Once we understand the root causes of certain circumstances that produce anger or the frustration that we've seen in this vicious cycle, we can be more aware of changes that need to follow in order to break the curse and redesign our life's environment and experiences. When we choose not to let go, we give things life to live, grow and fester, hindering our ability to grow ourselves. Trust that by sacrificing this, it will allow you to accomplish, "THAT." *Fill in the prompt below.*

If I sacrifice...

_____

_____

_____

I will be able to accomplish...

_____

_____

_____

Setting Your Declaration

Once you write your desire down on paper, announce it to the world and give a date to what you are trying to accomplish it continues to increase its chances of actually taking place. For everything that you desire I want you to set a date to it and commit to the activity during the process in order to see it through.

Whatever it is that you are carrying, whatever weight is holding your ship back from moving through the seas of realization and transformation, and whatever you need to take out of your life that you recognize isn't taking care of you, it is time to declare a date and set the intention. Remember in chapter one when I mentioned that starting isn't the hard part, remaining committed once you experience challenges is the real challenge and where most people stop right there at the brink of achieving everything they desire?

The best way to create an environment of success in your life and around your activity, is to partner each activity with a boundary in order to create barriers from people, distractions and anything that comes to interfere with what you are working to accomplish.

With every step, it is important to have three boundaries that can secure it and keep it in place. A boundary in my opinion is simply a tool and method of protecting what is that you want so that nothing or anyone can interfere with the focus required to achieve what you are working towards. In the activity below, let's map out your declaration roadmap.

What are 1-3 miracles you are working on accomplishing this quarter (next three months):

_____

_____

_____

For the miracles that you are working on, what is the specific date that you want it to be accomplished within that three month period:

_____

_____

_____

For each specific miracle, what are 3 activities that you need to commit to so daily so you can accomplish it by the specific date:

_____

_____

_____

For each specific activity, what are three boundaries you need to set in place with people, your space or environments so that you are not distracted by anything:

———————————————————————

———————————————————————

———————————————————————

Once you set the intention, write it down, declare a date and announce it to the world, it increases your chances of success in any area. You have set your intention, you've written it down and now you know what you need to do and what it will take; it's up to you to execute and through every challenge remember to counter it with grace as you keep moving forward.

Wrap Your ARM Around The Anger

When you are experiencing any emotion, the first response that most people have is to give someone a hug and embrace them. I believe the same should be true as we are experiencing our own set of emotions internally and for us to begin wrapping our ARM around the emotion, especially the anger and frustration that we may experience.

A. Address your feelings

As we've discussed throughout the pages in this book, once you feel it, acknowledge it and address whatever feeling it is that you are experiencing. Stop suffering in silence because you are not alone in this journey out at sea. Call a friend, peer or a professional and explain what you are feeling following the exercises that we shared with you in the earlier pages.

R. Remind yourself of who you are and what you bring to the world

Throughout this chapter we've helped you understand who you are and how significant your wants, desires and emotions are. You matter and remember this through the emotion, which will help you identify the next steps that need to happen in order for you to experience something more positive. Affirm yourself consistently and commit to practicing a self care activity that brings you joy and peace.

M. Map out the possibilities

The pain is temporary, but the possibilities are endless for your life if you just believe and continue to work on yourself. You can accomplish anything you want and desire. It just takes a bit of belief, a lot of courage with a hint of grace as your counter punch.

When I am experiencing a challenging experience I always try to remember the quote, "it takes many years to become an overnight wonder." In this battle that we are experiencing daily, it is up to you to prevail, all it takes is faith. You got this!

Know More to Jump The Rope

*Creating a Future Route Takes Being Released From Past
Wrongdoings*

- To be free of our past requires clarity in where we are
  going in the future.

- Ask Yourself: "What baggage am I holding on to
  right now that doesn't belong where I am working
  on going?"

Setting Deadlines For Yourself is a Declaration

- Setting arbitrary goals, don't allow us to reach a point
  of transformation where we are truly proud of ourselves. For each step you want to accomplish as a
  part of this healing journey, put a date next to it
  and re-work the activities so you can reach that goal
  intentionally.

Commit to Winning The Battles of Today to Conquer the War of Tomorrow

- I heard a quote once that stated; "It took me twenty years to become an overnight success." The same applies to the journey of transformation and healing. Commit to celebrating your smaller wins each day.

- Ask Yourself: "What wins have I had recently that I overlooked that I should be proud of?"

Feelings, Reflections and Actions

Use the pages below to write your feelings or reflections from the chapter or take this time to write out your action plan to begin YOUR BECOMING JOURNEY.

_____

_____

_____

_____

_____

_____

_____

_____

_____

_____

_____

_____

_____

_____

_____

_____

_____

_____

_____

_____

_____

_____

_____

_____

_____

_____

_____

_____

_____

_____

_____

_____

_____

_____

_____

_____

_____

_____

_____

_____

_____

_____

_____

_____

_____

_____

_____

_____

_____

_____

_____

_____

_____

_____

Chapter 3

FALLING IN LOVE WITH ME

"We sabotage the great things in our lives because deep down we don't feel worthy of having the great things." - Taressa Riazzi

I believe one of life's greatest mysteries that many of us have yet to realize is answering the question, "who am I really?" For so long our identities have been attached to our professional or personal titles rather than our contributions, values, and desires in life. People will ask for an introduction and you are quick to say, "I am the mother of, wife of, CEO or Manager of," rather than being in tune with the beautiful attributes that are a bit harder to quantify such as your giving heart, discerning spirit, or commitment to seeing other people happy even if at times it means sacrificing your wants and desires.

We have categorized our value to be the spouse, the parent or the professional rather than taking a focus on understanding who the actual person is inside of the image we've created for the world. As the opening quote states, "we sabotage the great things in our lives because deep down we don't feel worthy of having great things." We are experts at starting and have all the strength to withstand any blow, but it is our own fears, insecurities and self limiting beliefs that lead to us self sabotaging our own ship which leads to it sinking into shame, disappointment and the feeling of not being worthy of reaching the destination that we set our sail towards at the beginning.

We must begin to make a conscious effort to no longer set ourselves on fire so other people can feel warm around you. Choosing you and being true in what you need, want and desire is necessary to creating a life that God continues to bless. What I recognized when I wasn't making the choice is that I continued to have thoughts of taking my own life because I thought my life was expendable and not valuable. I want to be the first to tell you that your life has meaning and what you're going through is the necessary test so that you can continue to be blessed. You can no longer minimize your wants, dreams, and desires so others can feel comfortable and accepting of the decisions that you are choosing to make, which is best for you. One question that I urge you to ask before you bring your boat to ruin is, "Is this thought, feeling, or circumstance serving my future self or is it just fear that's running wild in my mind?" Once you take time to identify what it may be, it's up to you to choose the "next best move," by filling the holes of disbelief in your boat and continuing forward on your journey.

For years as I was working to build the JUMP brand, I battled with this so frequently and instead of believing in that inner song that continued to play on repeat in my mind, I choose to silence the beautiful melody with getting a second full time job, because I thought working harder would allow me to go higher. For the time I was, "working harder," my health took a massive decline which ultimately didn't allow me to go any higher or further, but each hour that I committed to working someone else's dream was an hour that I lost in my life committing to my own dream. In the last chapter, I had you write out a few goals that you were working towards accomplishing in the next three months and you wrote down the declaration roadmap so that you can minimize the distractions by creating boundaries. Within the 5-10 minutes it took you to read that section, it gave you a clear roadmap and picture on what you needed to not do next, but what you are capable of doing right now.

The harder truth is how long have you either known about those goals but haven't taken action or not known about the goals that you wrote because of all of the "responsibilities, distractions, and people," you're allowing to take you further from your dream which isn't allowing you to go higher up in your purpose. Each "choice" that you say YES to ultimately is screaming NO to your calling if it doesn't align with the map that you are following. By consistently asking yourself the question of, is the thought, feeling, or circumstance serving my future self or is just fear that's running wild in my mind, you will be able to better assess each opportunity, decision and action that you take in order for you to be progressive and not regressive.

The truth is, whether we are intentional or not about the actions, we all have goals that we have either mentioned, written down or thought in our head to accomplish one day. Each day that we wait and allow excuses to empower our procrastination, our dreams sit dormant in our minds and spirits awaiting our attention and intention. Recognize that no failure, pain, heartache or challenge is stronger than the calling that's been put onto your life and you have the ability to accomplish anything you desire in this world. Replace self sabotage with a system of commitment and consistency and remove all doubt and replace it with continued discipline and focus as you pursue what is already yours in this world.

When we break down what self sabotage really means and represents, it simply is a defense mechanism that protects us from being vulnerable and allowing people to see who we are at the core. Remember that there is velocity and your vulnerability and the more honest that you are first with yourself, the easier it will be to stand up with courage and be vulnerable with others that you may encounter.

The central theme of the idea of jumping into your destiny and manifesting your success is all about replacing any doubt and fear with the key characteristic of courage. Follow these steps below to have a counteractive method once sabotage starts to creep through the walls of your ship while you're out at sea.

Visualize The Goal

Think of the initial goal that you want to accomplish even if you don't believe it is possible. I want you to open your journal or create a google document and type it out vividly where you can almost see it. I want you to record yourself reading it and then save that recording on your phone. I want you to print out the goal and post it somewhere you see it every day you wake up in the morning. Every night before you go to bed, watch the video you recorded and remember what you're working towards every single day and through every challenge remember the feeling of reading it and what it would be like to accomplish that very thing.

Reflect On Your Ability

Write down on another sheet of paper, and title it, "my self sabotage won't win today." Write down all of the negative feelings that you currently have and the beliefs that you are feeling consistently and regularly about accomplishing that very goal. On another sheet of paper, write, title it, "I will win today." On this sheet of paper write down all of the characteristics, people or abilities you do possess that will help you accomplish the goal. Take 20-30 seconds encouraging or affirming yourself as you look at the list of positive traits and then take out a match and set the first list on fire and scream, "My self sabotage won't win today." Starting today, you will burn away any disbelief and thoughts that no longer serve you and begin to embrace all that you do possess because you have everything that you need inside already.

Be Aware of When it Arrives

We discussed self awareness in the previous chapter and when we are feeling a bit off or in a state of disbelief we must still use the same tips that we discussed earlier in order to be aware when self sabotage is creeping in our ship. Remember, nothing will stop you from accomplishing what you desire, so be aware of the things listed below so you can know when to course correct:

- You self generate stress (starting more projects than you can complete)

- You expect yourself to succeed in making life changes without designating any time or mental space to accomplish them.

- You ignore warning signs that you need a break

- You hold yourself back due to "I can't thoughts"

- You work on low priority tasks but leave high priority tasks undone

If you see any of these happening above, it's time for you to go back to the list that you wrote earlier and recreate that activity and take action. Don't let your self sabotage win because you are in control of your life.

Take Action and Embrace Change

Beginning today, commit to no longer allowing past issues, beliefs or curses to define who you are today. This is your story and you are the author of your destiny. Use what you've experienced as motivation to fuel your mission and remove the judgment and shame because you are worthy of love, success, joy, peace and all of the desires that you envision for your life.

Think of the goal consistently and keep it in front of you always. Every time you accomplish a goal, recreate another document and record another video so you can never forget what you are working towards. Map out your plan, take action and commit to your process when challenges arise.

Practicing Self Compassion

Once you make the choice, the decisions that follow are easier to follow. As we are practicing self compassion and love, it is important for us to be committed to choosing forgiveness so that the decisions that follow support and empower us rather than create distance further away from the destination that we have our compass set on.

Choose Forgiveness

T.D. Jakes quoted that, "I think the first step is to understand that forgiveness does not exonerate the perpetrator. Forgiveness liberates the victim and it's a gift you give yourself." It's important for you to forgive by acknowledging the hurt, understanding how it affected you, accepting what was done as well as what was caused and being committed to the process of repairing, learning and healing. Forgiveness is a journey that will take you through a process of strengthening who you are in order for you to be able to better navigate circumstances and situations that mirror what you once experienced.

Create a Growth Mindset

Your perspective in your mind creates the reality on the path towards accomplishing your mission, so it is important that you create a growth mindset by seeing every challenge as an opportunity for learning, growth and development. As you are committing to reflecting on a daily basis, look at where you could have grown as well as identifying opportunities to celebrate, honor and reward your actions. As a part of your daily reflection, one question that should always be answered is, "What did I learn, gain, and experience today that made me better?" If you were to commit to doing this for 365 days, you could look back and recognize 365 potential points of reference of growth at the end of the year.

Exercise Gratitude Always

Gratitude should be a practice that we commit to every single day, because every day we wake up is a blessing. When we exercise gratitude it allows us to create a more grounded and peaceful environment as well as improving the relationships that we have with others in our lives. As a part of your daily journaling exercise, write down 3-5 things that you are grateful for each day. I believe as life continues, responsibilities come in and different challenges are thrown at us, we forget about all of the many opportunities in our lives to celebrate and be grateful for. Exercise gratitude always and daily.

Pour In Kindness Pour Out Love

In Ephesians 4:32, scripture tells us, "Be kind and compassionate to one another, forgiving others, just as in Chris God forgave you." I believe this should be a value that if we all embodied it would allow us to create better experiences and empower better relationships with the people that we encounter. It is said that what you appreciate, will appreciate; so appreciate who you are and what you pour into yourself, so that you can pour out something magical into the world. Be the person that makes every person special, loved, supported and seen and this same response will be reciprocated back to you as well. I challenge you to ask this question, "If you were to look at how you treated the last 5 people you encountered, what would that say about who you are as a person?" I urge you to be more mindful in your experiences with others because it serves as a reflection to who you are yourself.

The Journey of Patterns

According to mental health professionals and researchers, journaling is one of the most recommended tools to have a clearer mind and a happier life. In the different experiences that we encounter, keeping a journal helps you identify patterns of behavior that may lead to shame, sabotage, grief and this will allow you to track the pattern and try new ways of acting that promotes the possibilities and doesn't recreate the pain.

If you were to trace your decisions, choices and actions over the last week and continue to do that over a course of 4 more months, where would you end up? Would you be proud of that place and of the experiences that you have left people with? If you begin to reflect on where this will end up, and if you're not proud, then it's time for you to alter the course now and begin acting and making decisions in a way that promotes the ending that you want to create.

Ask yourself this question, "What actions need to be in my behavioral pattern that can get me to where I desire to be in 6 months? What do I need to change now?"

When we begin to recreate this journey of patterns that we are experiencing it allows us to be much more proactive in our journey as well as intentional with where we will end up. If we want to recreate our lives, it starts with understanding our patterns, making the necessary adjustments and getting back on track.

Trigger Mastery

In psychology, it is said that a "trigger," is a stimulus that causes a painful memory to resource. Anything may cause a person to recall a traumatic experience such as an image, video or less obvious things such as songs, odors or even colors could trigger someone based upon their experiences. It is the same with you and when we begin to listen to our body, acknowledge our feelings, create space within and around us and turn each negative emotion into positive action it will allow us to create a more positive approach when dealing with certain triggers that we may naturally experience.

Listen to Your Body

When we are listening to our bodies, it means that we are mindful and fully aware of how we feel and when things feel a bit off or different than normal. Whether you are stressed, feel tension in a specific area in your body or maybe just feel frustrated or a bit irritable; listening to your body is critical when we are triggered in any way. Take a moment to write down what your body is saying to you and what that represents. Too often we aren't checking in with ourselves because we feel the need to keep going. If you are feeling something that isn't normal, stop to take time and reflect on what you are feeling as well as what you may need moving forward.

Acknowledge Your feelings

Once you know what your body is saying, I want you to tell your body thank you for communicating that to you and give yourself a pat on the back for being intentional with giving yourself grace. Don't be judgmental or fill yourself up with more shame, accept the feelings as they exist without trying to suppress or push them back, down or away. We often are quick to feel, and even quicker to hide or bury our feelings because we don't feel like we have the time, space or support to experience them as they exist. Give yourself a moment to experience and feel and acknowledge what you believe is best moving forward. Before you can create the best course of action, it is important for you to acknowledge what is actually going on in your ship.

Create Space Within and Around You

Creating space and setting boundaries are simply the lines we draw for ourselves in terms of our level of comfort around others so that we can get the things that we need. Whether it is physical contact, verbal interactions or specific boundaries that will allow you to have the environment necessary to promote what you need once you are experiencing triggers and feelings that you're navigating through. In these spaces it is important to visualize and give a name to your limits so that your capacity tank isn't overflowing.

Just because you have the ability to answer a phone call or text, doesn't mean emotionally that you have the capacity. Just because you have the ability to go out with friends, doesn't mean you are in a place mentally or physically where you have the capacity. So don't only think about your ability to do something, think about if you really want to hold space for that effort so that you can get the things that you also need.

During these spaces where you need space and are actively creating boundaries, it is important for you to openly communicate what you need, and be sure to enforce and uphold those boundaries with the people around you so that you can receive what you need in this period of time.

Having the courage to say no and taking time for yourself is necessary for ensuring that your cup is full and not depleted when it is time to show up for the dream that you are working towards.

Negative Emotion, Positive Action

Throughout this whole chapter we've explored how to transfer the negative emotions that we experience into positive action. Everything that we've explored comes down to having the courage as well as complimenting it with the growth mindset in order for you to be brave with boundaries so that you can receive the very things that you desire in your life. Use the questions provided on the next page for further reflection and self assessment. I am excited to see you in the next chapter!

Know More to Jump The Rope

Replacing All Self Doubt Statements With Self-Courage Affirmations

- Remove any "I can't" thought to thoughts that are affirming what you can, will and have the capacity to do. Remember, you are worthy and deserving of everything you are working towards.

- Ask yourself: "How can I honor myself today with my words and actions?"

Pay Attention To The "Take a Break" Signs Your Body is Giving Off

- Listen to your body and don't ignore warning signs that you need a break.

- Ask yourself: "What can I do today that is going to make me happy where I can express myself freely?"

Commit to High Priority Activities ONLY

- Every moment you work on low priority tasks you

leave high priority action steps undone.

- Ask yourself: "What are the tasks that I can complete today that will help me get one step closer to where I know I deserve to be?"

Feelings, Reflections and Actions

Use the pages below to write your feelings or reflections from the chapter or take this time to write out your action plan to begin YOUR BECOMING JOURNEY.

_____

_____

_____

_____

_____

_____

_____

_____

_____

_____

_____

_____

_____

_____

Chapter 4

THE CONFIDENCE CURVE

"Surrendering to who you really are and why you are here may very well change the world." - Maria Flynn

Why is it so hard to be honest? So hard to let your guard down with the people in your life and allow them to accept you for who you truly are at all times? Why can't we just fully express our feelings, intentions, wants and desires with all people we come in contact with whether they are good or bad? Wouldn't that be easier for us all, to just be real, open and courageous enough to share the experience that we would desire to have in this interaction. I believe it would be something special when we recognized the power in integrity and the peace that comes with honesty. The integrity of authenticity where we give ourselves the chance to be who we were designed to be free of judgment, shame and without any care towards the opinions of the world.

Why does it feel like we are rehearsing the truth and fluently flowing out lies in our conversations, throughout our relationships and in the midst of our interactions. Has the world made it okay to lie, is telling the truth so challenging, or are we so insecure or unsure about who we truly are that it leads us to painting a picture and showing the world, while altering the most beautiful colors of ourselves in the process. The emotions that we experience, the perspectives that challenge status quo, the desires that we have inside that we sometimes don't feel comfortable to share with the world, or even our deepest fears that we recognize may push people away.

I'll tell you what honesty represents; strength, courage and power. Honesty represents legacy and is the seed we plant that waters the reputation that we will leave when our body returns back to the dirt. Integrity, in all things, is the natural ingredient that is absolutely necessary as we prepare to cook our calling and become all things that we are intended to become.

This virus of lies that we have allowed to spread through our relationships, business interactions and within ourselves is killing the very nature that God intended for us to live out here on earth. It is leading to beautiful relationships burning, innovative companies ending, and the potential of powerful people being destroyed. This virus, however, has a longer term approach on your wellbeing and is different than a gunshot, because it takes time to fester and slowly eat away at your character, reputation and everything that was once healthy and pure over time becomes manipulative, cold, while lacking empathy and compassion.

I've realized this virus has found its way to me too many times throughout my life, not knowing its origin but continuing to know the catalyst for its rapid growth and internal destruction. Yet like most diseases and killers in the African American culture, it is our diets and choices that allow our bodies to internally decay leading to our dreams and callings being slowly taken from the world. Through any season of transformation, it's not always about what you are doing that makes the most difference, it often is about what you choose to sacrifice out of your diet and lifestyle that make all the difference. It's about not sacrificing the people in our life that continue to have a hold on you and you refuse to set boundaries, cut chords while recognizing where you are going can no longer have them to be a part of your new mission.

It is about changing your pallet of conversation and what you consume. It is about taking accountability for all of your actions, but before an action takes place, being considerate of the other person and how that would affect their experience. It is about sharing freely, communicating honestly, and being willing to make adjustments that will cause you to get back in balance and in alignment with who God is intending for you to be. It is about being true to your word, honoring your commitments with excellence and understanding that apologies don't hold any value without change in behavior, action and perspective. What is required may bring temporary discomfort, but is essential for long term development of what has the potential to be built and developed.

The hardest pill that I've had to swallow is the pill of lack alignment and balance, when I recognize who I communicate that I am, is so far from what my actions have been communicating for years. Are you actually that person you admire or deep down are there things about you that you remain ashamed of, hidden or doubt? There's been times where we didn't have the support and like me, we listen to the coach, the YouTube Video, and all the so-called experts tell us the same things we know deep down inside of us already, confirming all of our perspectives and things we already know to be true. This leads us to wanting to quit, feeling a sense of being less loved and lacking value. To be courageous allows us to be confident in ourselves as long as we remain committed.

I could blame my upbringing, my influences, the world around me and so many things, but that would exonerate me from the responsibility that I have on my life and the choices that I still had the free will to make. The root may be your history and what you've been through, but the responsibility is now which will take you to where you need to be. I have to stop blaming my circumstance for the situations I knew would be created from my choices.

The only question that matters is not where did this begin, but when does this end? Once you are aware of what your actions have caused, it is the mark of a good man, to change them immediately before the ripple of pride and pain continue. Once you know the problems, fix it and figure out the solutions immediately so that you can create better experiences with the time you still have left in this world. It is not about putting a shield up from your insecurities, flaws, flaws, mistakes, choices and current circumstances, because when you do, the world is not allowed to support you and you continue to suffer alone. Rather being alone through this journey of finding your path and walking your road, you must allow the world to see you for who you truly are, where you are, because it allows God to position people in your life that can really help, mold and benefit you towards not recreating the cycle of pain and disappointment.

Life is not about having all of the answers to share with people, it is about sharing with people the questions that you have about life, in order for us to unify and work through the answers together. Integrity is the foundation to living a peaceful and joyful life, not opportunities, not people, not location, or resources. It is integrity because it allows you to be free, walk freely and be the actual person that you are inside, while aligning your choices, wants, desires, relationships and opportunities with that very person.

If you continue to minimize your wants, desires, and not be mindful of who you are, it doesn't matter how much the world gives you, God will never grant you what is promised until you stand courageous in your power by first being honest with yourself. It is okay to not want the relationship anymore that you've invested so much into. It is okay to remove friends out of your life that have been there for so long and you have history with. It is okay to not be in the best financial position and it's also okay to not know how to get yourself out of it. It is okay not to have everything together and to have a bit of debt and outstanding bills.

It is okay to not want to be married at that specific time or to change your mind throughout life's experiences. It is okay to say no to things you actually don't want to do or to not commit to things you know won't bring you peace or joy. It is okay to change careers, to go back to school, or to leave the country without letting anyone know. It is okay to make choices that make you happy and bring you joy; but it is not okay to lie, manipulate, and be dishonest through your pursuit of choosing what happiness looks like to you. What you want in life will threaten and interfere with what others want for you and with you; but how you get what you truly want is by setting boundaries, communicating honestly, moving with consideration and compassion and reflecting before revealing any desire.

- Because I have failed, does not make me a failure.

- Because I have lost, does not make me a loser.

- Because I don't have the answer, does not make me less worthy or deserving of asking the question.

Your lack, flaw, insecurity, and gap in your life is what is holding you back from who you are called to be and what you are deserving of experiencing. This same lack, flaw, insecurity, and gap in your life will serve as your superpower, all it takes is sharing, being willing to receive assistance and support, being open with asking the right questions, and remaining committed to the process that it takes to filling the gap and at the same time it will fill your love tank. Do not walk in shame for what you have done, who you have been, and what you've caused or created.

- Give yourself grace to fall, forgive yourself through mistakes, and smile at times where you are feeling unsuccessful.

- Plant your feet strong in the cement of integrity and do not waiver on your values and character.

- Silence the noise around you in order to begin listening to the voice inside of you.

- Reflect on the responsibilities prior to making any commitment

- Through every interaction, walk with compassion, love, grace and consideration

- Communicate your wants and needs clearly while being willing to set boundaries or have them set with you

- Think about the consequence of your action, before you act.

- Show love, give love and be love always

- Be comfortable being in temporary discomfort, because it serves as the strength to develop who you are

Integrity and authenticity is the foundation to life's greatest mystery as we continue to ask ourselves, who am I really? My prayer is that when you find the answer it is not too late and that you still have time to walk with that person for a while.

Mastering The Mistake

With every mistake comes the perspective gained in order to manifest miracles. Stop beating yourself up for falling, you are not alone in this journey of self actualization and transformation. In any mistake there are three steps to take every time and that is acknowledging the error, analyzing the potential outcomes and to commit to asking better questions.

Acknowledge the Error

Where did you fall short and where did the error take place in your life long experiment? Just as we learned in science class in high school, even if he has a strong hypothesis, based upon following the scientific method doesn't guarantee that the result after the experiment will be exactly how we expected. The same is true in life as well. We often are so attached to the result, that we don't honor and celebrate the process getting us a different outcome. Reflect on where the error took place as a part of the process and use this as an opportunity to learn instead of highlighting this as a loss.

Analyze The Potential Outcomes

When we lose, it only gives you an understanding on how to win the next time. Once you've acknowledged the errors that have occurred, take time to understand the potential outcomes if you would have done a few things differently. You are one to two moves away from being in the exact position that you need to be, but it takes reflection and analyzing history in order to create a better future. Complete the statement below.

If I would have done

_____

_____

_____

the results could have potentially been

_____

_____

_____

Each time you are analyzing the next step, complete the statement below so you can see all of the possibilities.

Ask Better Questions

Stop seeking answers and commit to asking better questions and your transformation will be realized. Through the process of acknowledging errors and analyzing the potential outcomes, it's important to ask questions that will help fill gaps, curve any challenge that you may be experiencing, and help you understand what is the best course of action moving forward. As a part of your daily reflection exercises, ask one question in the morning that you can actively take time learning or seeking out the answer. Whether through books, podcast, coaching, mentorship the questions that you seek will help you identify the resources you need to fill any gap that may be causing friction on your journey.

Don't Believe Everything You Think

In earlier chapters we discussed the importance of self regulation in the pursuit of being more emotionally intelligent and intuitive. As a part of this practice studies have shown that mindfulness can help us increase our ability to regulate emotions, decrease stress, anxiety and depression.

Be Mindful of Your Thoughts

Recognizing our thoughts and where they are leading us is one of the first steps to changing our relationships to them. Throughout this book we've helped you understand the importance of identifying your thoughts and being mindful of your feelings and emotions. Remain intentional in your efforts to cultivate awareness and give attention to the thoughts, feelings and sensations as they arise without being judgmental but curious as you continue to explore who you are and what it is that you desire.

Surround Yourself With Positivity

Who are people that you surround yourself around that make you feel happy, free to be yourself and a sense of peace that you enjoy? Also reflect on who people are when you are around them, it makes you feel discomfort, suffocated and a sense of tension and unease. Whether you believe it or not, your relationships are the breadcrumbs to your destiny and play a major role in cultivating the life that you envision for yourself. Surround yourself with happy individuals who motivate you to become better and to believe in the importance of positivity. Align yourself with individuals that mirror your values and beliefs and have similar drive towards their goals and dreams as well. If it does not serve you, it can not sit with you, and you must continue to surround yourself with people who can advance you forward and not lead to disconnecting you from your destiny.

Have The Courage to Speak Up For Yourself

Having the courage to speak up for yourself is important when informing those around you about what you feel, think and are experiencing while engaging with them. Whether people agree or not, is completely, but it is not okay to waiver on your beliefs, values, perspectives to make others feel comfortable. Don't feel the need to censor yourself and if you are misunderstood be sure to ask questions in order to empathize as well as understand. Your answers are formed from your education and experience and they are significant.

Activate Your Inner Authenticity

Who you are, what you want and where you want to go matters and the world knows it. As a part of you activating your inner authenticity, it's important to lay a proper foundation with core values being concrete.

Identify Your Core Values

Core values are the foundation that you should build your life on before anything else. Whether it is your faith, your ability to be integral and honest, or how you believe relationships should operate; it is important that each interaction in your life is measured by your core values. What do you value, want and believe in your life and how are you ensuring that you don't waiver on any of these to appease other people in your life?

Assessing relationships with core values is effective because you are looking at character traits rather than abilities and resources they can provide you. Be open to losing out on deals, missing opportunities and prolonging purpose, in order to align yourself with people and environments that are mirrors of what you value most at the core.

Believe in Yourself

The journey that we've been on throughout the pages of JUMP, I hope have given you the strength, knowledge and courage to take action immediately. All of the words and tactics would mean nothing if at the core you didn't believe in the calling that's been put onto your life. You are so valuable, worthy and deserving of everything you are wanting to experience, all it takes is a lot of faith and grace and I promise you'll be able to get to any place that you desire. Believe every day that you can prevail past pain, you can hurdle over trials, and you can crack through the ceilings of any negative circumstances. You are equipped with the knowledge and resources necessary to become anything you desire, all it takes is grit, grace and for you to remember the gift that you've put on this world to accomplish. Remember who you are and believe in what you have already inside of you.

Know More to Jump The Rope

Confidence is Key to a Happy and Fulfilling Life

- The Confidence journey is just that, a journey so take it slow and remember to honor yourself consistently.

- Ask yourself: "What are the activities that make me happy when I am doing them?"

Relationships Are What Makes Life Rich

- The relationships that we have or don't have will determine where we end up in our lives. Determine where you want to go and recruit the people that can help you get there.

- Ask yourself: " What relationships in my life are valuable and can help me pull off the big win in my life?"

Accepting Yourself is To Love Yourself

- When you begin to accept who you are and embrace your imperfections, this is a major step into falling in love with yourself.

- Ask yourself: " What things about myself do I need to accept about myself that are a part of who I am?

Feelings, Reflections and Actions

Use the pages below to write your feelings or reflections from the chapter or take this time to write out your action plan to begin YOUR BECOMING JOURNEY.

_____

_____

_____

_____

_____

_____

_____

_____

_____

_____

_____

_____

_____

Chapter 5

PREPARING YOUR LANDING

"Women, if the soul of the nation is to be saved, I believe you must become its soul." - Coretta Scott King

Writing this book was a journey, forcing me to unpack, unravel and understand who I was even more. Recognizing how some of the stories and experiences in my life have affected me helped me create resources for you to navigate some of the tragedies that I had to experience on my own.

Before I was prepared to communicate to you in a way where you could understand, receive and commit to the actions techniques, I needed to be sure that my journey was complete and that I had mastered the areas I was teaching and sharing with you throughout the various chapters.

Throughout this book, we've covered the importance of taking that first leap, preparing to jump, courage, character, consistency, and how this collection of attributes serves as the ingredients that help us arrive at the shore of success.

If you don't walk away with anything but one thing, it would be that you have everything you already need at your disposal, and there are no gadgets, technology, education, or experience that you need to embark on the journey that you've been called to lead.

All it will take is for you to dive deeper and begin to commit to the action steps that you've been prolonging and procrastinating from doing for so long. It is your mission to accomplish the very thing that you've been called to perform because there are people out in this world waiting for you to land on that tarmac so that they can hear your testimony and use your techniques to be able to change their life.

Your story matters, and the experiences you've communicated, and felt, either good or bad, are significant and will help shape and create ripples of impact throughout all the people you touch after reading the story. Think through the emotions you endured, the experiences that empowered you, and even the times when you felt alone. Use your account to be able to empathize with others and allow it to change lives. First, you change yours.

As we've explained, the challenge with any journey is not always at takeoff; the challenge lies with the challenges you encounter during the trip enabling the character to be created, while courage will remain a requirement.

Our final chapter is about celebrating your commitment through your flight while continuing to assist you as you prepare for your landing. I have taken many flights, and one thing is always the same; The landing is an essential part of the journey. You've done the work throughout your life and through the different exercises that we've had you commit to doing throughout this text.

You are more than prepared and equipped with the necessary knowledge and resources to go out there and empower your life while remaining committed to touching others as they work diligently to accomplish theirs. As we get closer to our final destination, the pilot will announce to all passengers that the plane is preparing for landing. At this announcement, it is communicated for each passenger to put their table trays up, sit their seats up, as well as close any larger electronic devices that cause a distraction to keep everyone safe and prepare them for a successful landing. As you prepare to land your plane, close any chapters that are not allowed to come into this next season. It's time for you to have crucial conversations with the necessary people who will be a part of this next journey or will not be part of it.

It's time to clean up your area and understands the things that you need to implement within your life, and the behaviors and the choices and the necessary actions that you need to begin committing to that will be necessary so that you can be entirely focused as you embark and try to enter into new levels and atmospheres.

Once the announcement is made, it's time to ease into the position where you drop your landing gear so that before you touch the ground, you can review the terrain to ensure that you have the proper speed, your plane is at the appropriate position, and you can propel your dream forward in a way that allows you to be safe and secure while also being able to slide into the necessary Gate.

This gate is all about unlocking your gift, your genius, as you commit to the grind necessary that will be required for you to accomplish the calling that has been put onto your life. Throughout this book, we have talked about the importance of understanding your emotions and feelings—but be sure that your values are the concrete you build your foundation on as you make this house of integrity and innovation.

Throughout these chapters, we've understood how you can prepare your crew as well as being mindful of the inner voice that serves as your compass so that you can continue to have a discerning spirit that will help you assess relationships, opportunities, or any choice or decision that we'll follow, throughout the different chapters. It's essential for you to have the courage to remain committed to the process and if any challenge that serves as a blow arises, you are to counteract that challenge and blow with grace and forgiveness.

One of the most potent pieces of these words is to practice self-care, commit to becoming emotionally intuitive and intelligent, and not self-sabotaging your success on the road to the shore of your destiny. I urge and challenge you to take action, review all the material that has been covered, reflect daily and use the journal activity so that you can continue to do temperature checks on where you are for you to remain committed, motivated, and disciplined on the path towards purpose.

You are deserving of love, worthy of winning, and will accomplish everything that you set out to accomplish, but all it takes is faith, belief—grit, and the hug and wrapping your arms around grace.

I am so thankful that you spent so much time with me through reading these chapters and words, and I'm grateful for what we've been able to share. I ask that this is not the end of your journey, but this is the beginning, and after you read this book, you leave a review on Amazon and join the masterclass described at the beginning of the book. Follow me on all social media outlets. But before you do any of that, it's time for you to jump and move your success so that you can manifest your dream. We'll see you next time.

Feelings, Reflections and Actions

Use the pages below to write your feelings or reflections from the chapter or take this time to write out your action plan to begin YOUR BECOMING JOURNEY.

_____

_____

_____

_____

_____

_____

_____

_____

_____

_____

_____

_____

_____

_____

_____

_____

_____

_____

_____

_____

_____

_____

_____

_____

_____

_____

_____

_____

_____

_____

_____

_____

_____

About Author

Bernadette Henry

Bernadette Henry is the founder and Chief Executive Officer of Make it FUN NYC, a lifestyle brand focused on getting fit physically and mentally. Recognized in national magazines and digital platforms, her exceptional exercise career gained her recognition on the Dr. Oz Show helped Henry to be named one of the most influential women in the health and wellness industry. Outside of growing her globally recognized organization, Bernadette works as a case manager in social work helping individuals with HIV/AIDS and mental disabilities ensuring they are able to live their lives a bit brighter. Proud wife and mother of three children, Bernadette currently lives in New York. To find more information about Bernadette Henry email her at info@makeitfunnyc.com.

Made in the USA
Middletown, DE
12 June 2023

32427011R00071